Teacher's note: Have children trace over the letter and colour the picture when the study of the focus letter is complete.

Channel

Trace over

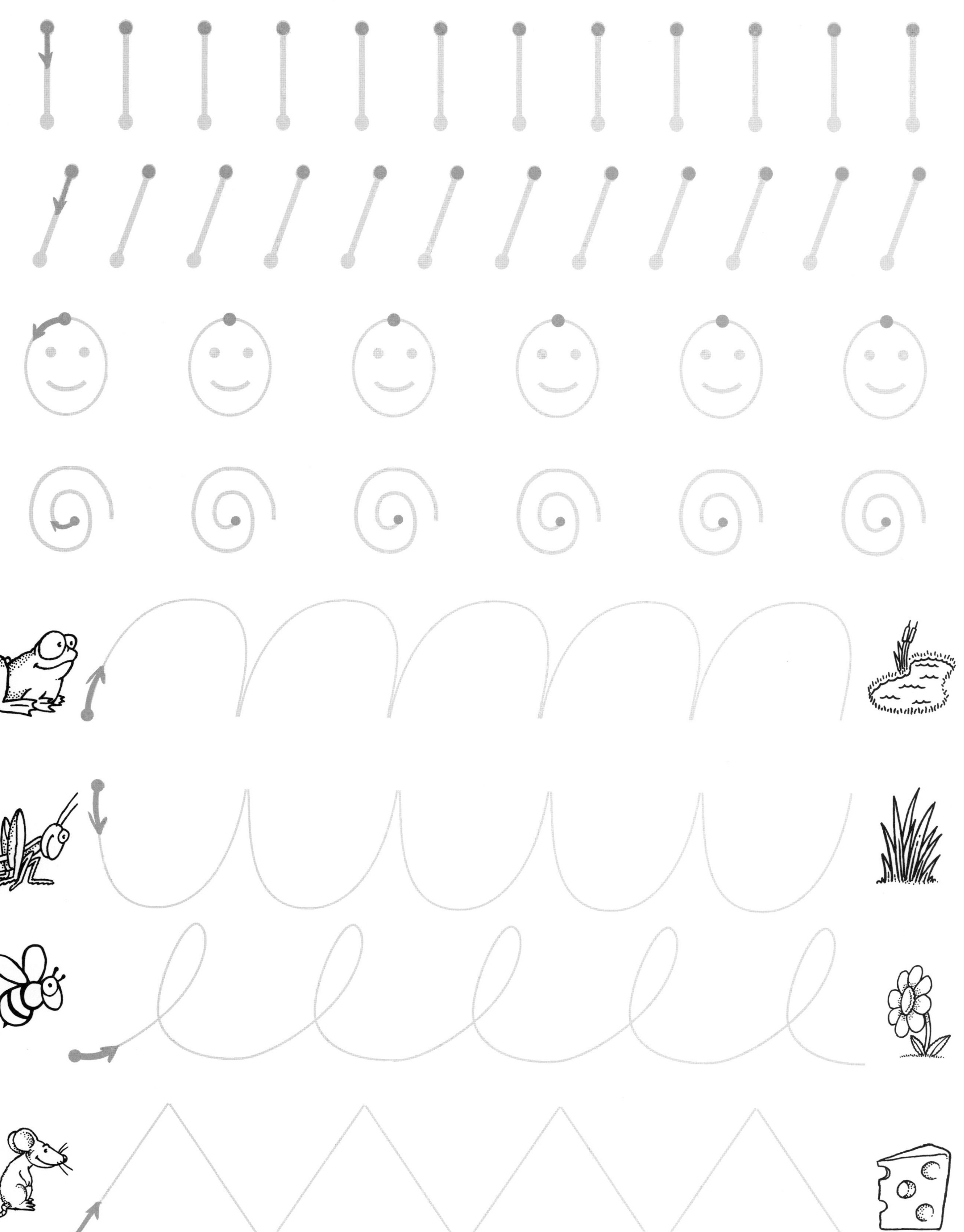

Channel

Trace over

a a a a a

Copy

a

Trace over

ant ant ant

Aa

Bb

Channel

b b b b b

Trace over

b b b b b

Copy

b

Trace over

bee bee bee

Channel

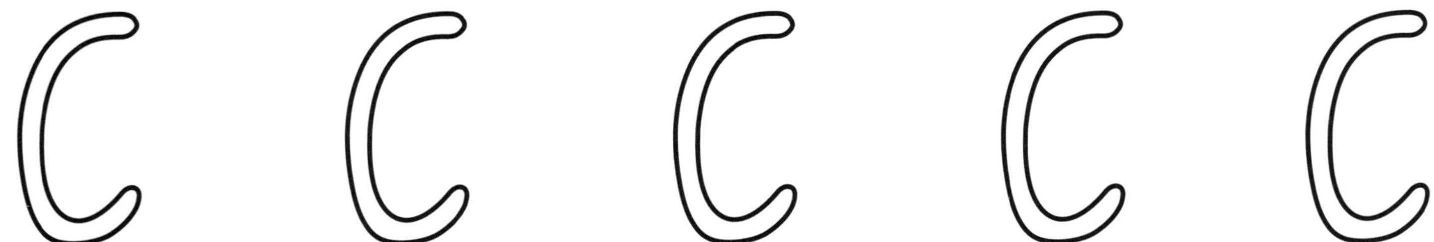

Trace over

c c c c c

Copy

c

Trace over

cake cake cake

Cc

Dd

Channel

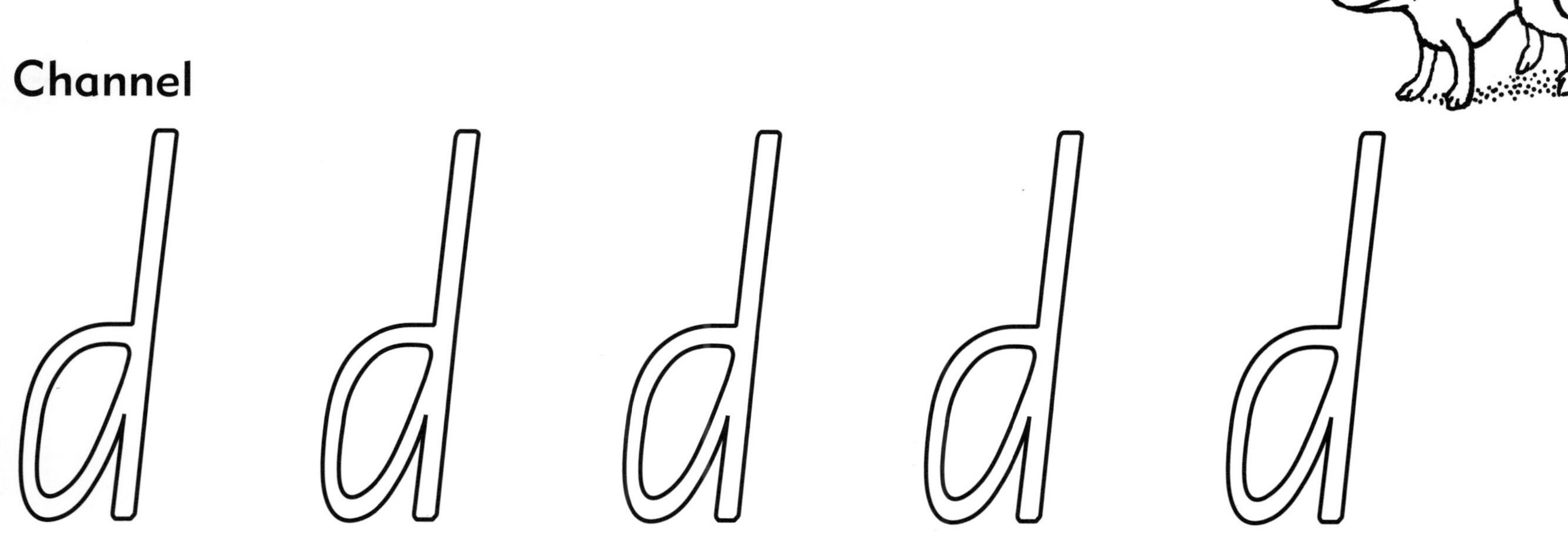

Trace over

d d d d d

Copy

d

Trace over

dog dog dog

Channel

e e e e e

Trace over

e e e e e

Copy

e

Trace over

ears ears ears

Ee

Ff

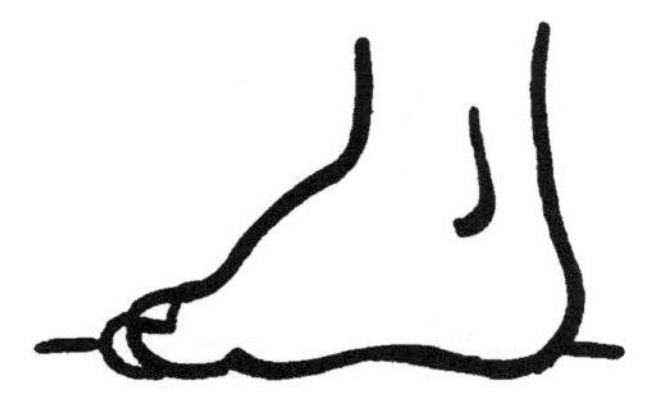

Channel

f f f f f

Trace over

f f f f f

Copy

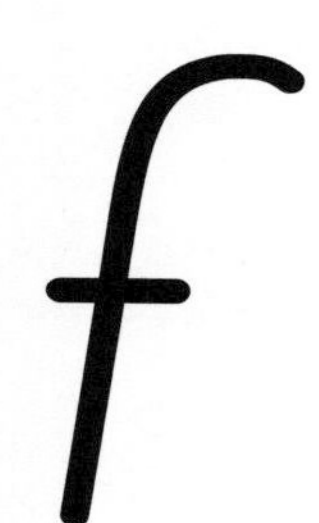

Trace over

foot foot foot

Channel

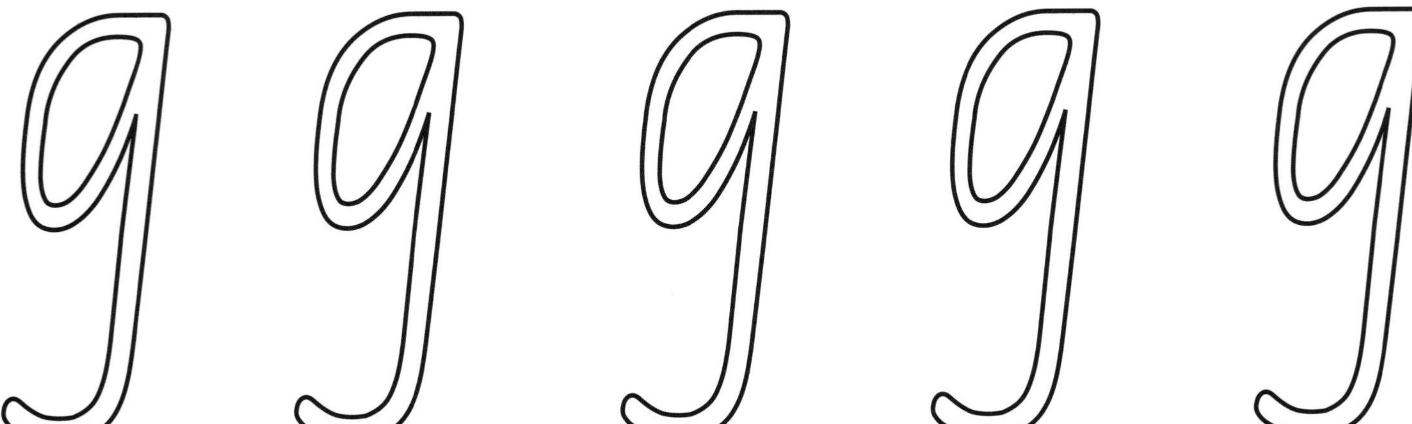

Trace over

g g g g g

Copy

g

Trace over

goat goat goat

Gg

Hh

Channel

Trace over

h h h h h

Copy

h

Trace over

hand hand hand

Channel

i i i i i

Trace over

i i i i i

Copy

i

Trace over

igloo igloo igloo

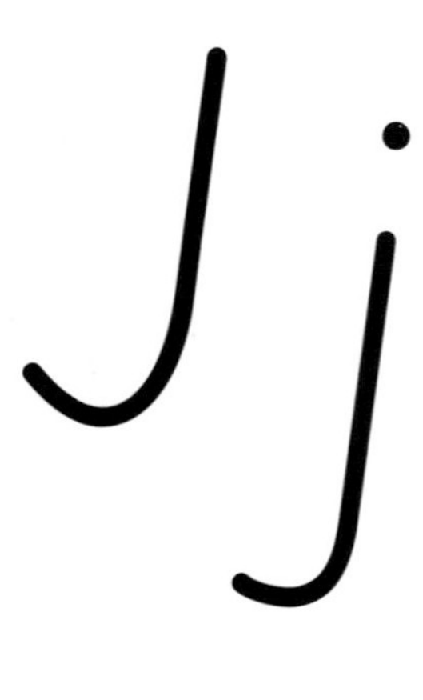

Channel

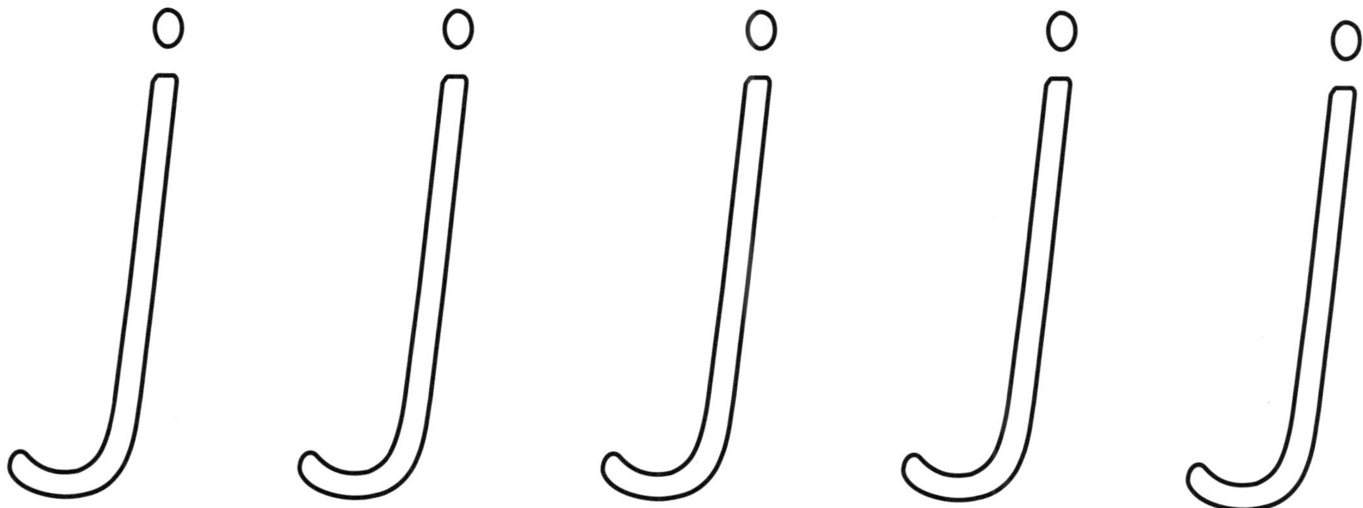

Trace over

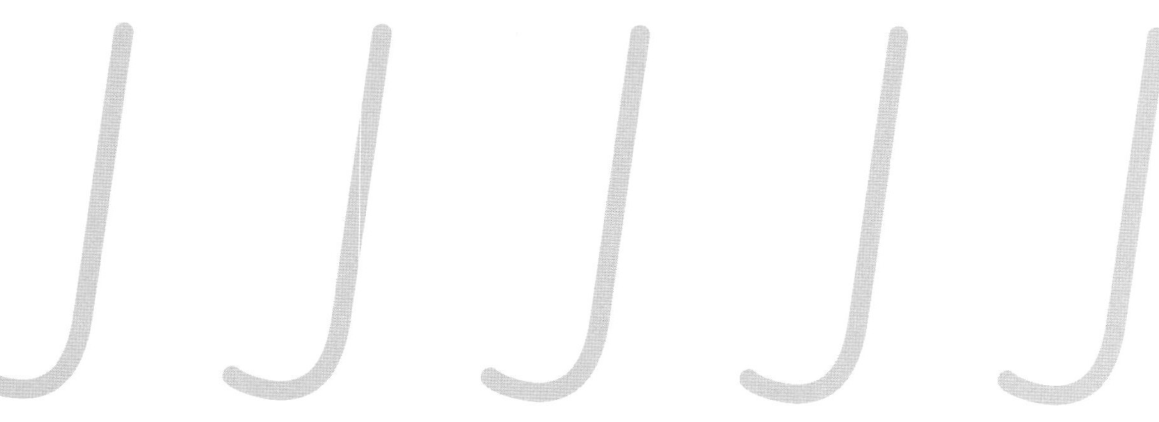

Copy

Trace over

jigsaw jigsaw

Channel

k k k k k

Trace over

k k k k k

Copy

k

Trace over

king king king

Kk

Channel

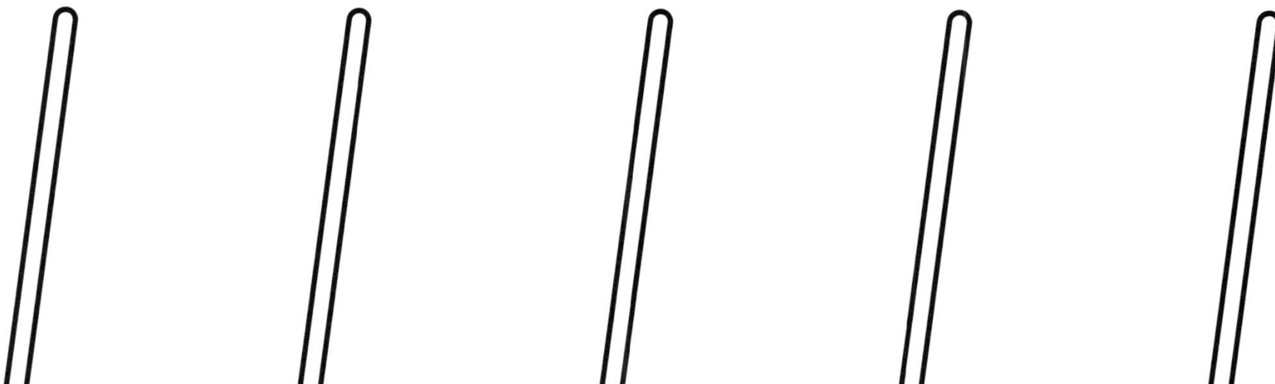

Trace over

Copy

Trace over

lips lips lips

Channel

m m m m

Trace over

m m m m

Copy

m

Trace over

mouse mouse

Mm

m

Nn

Channel

n n n n n

Trace over

n n n n n

Copy

n

Trace over

nest nest nest

Channel

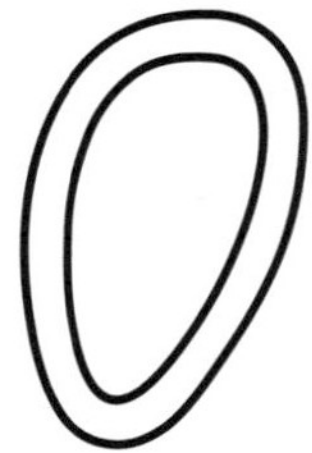 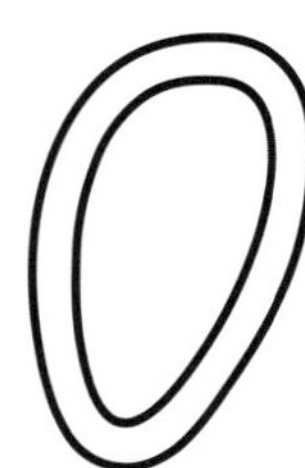 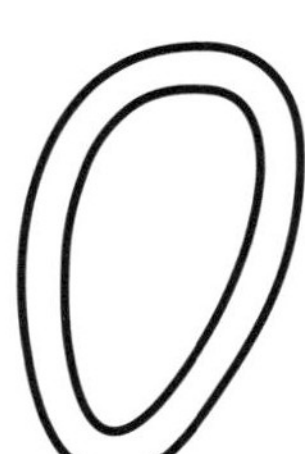 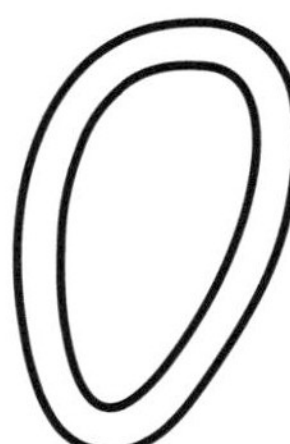 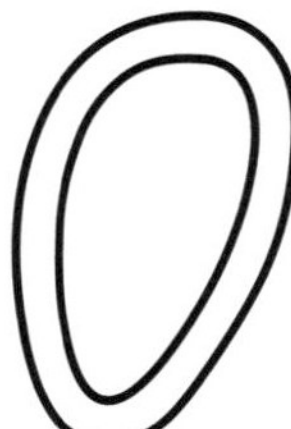

Trace over

o o o o o

Copy

o

Trace over

octopus octopus

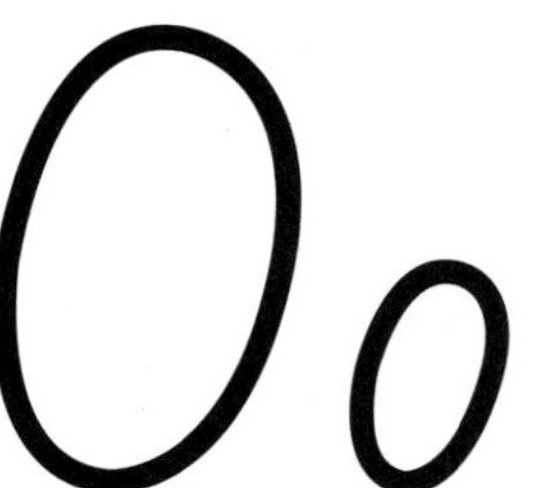

Pp

Channel

p p p p p

Trace over

p p p p p

Copy

Trace over

pig pig pig

Channel

q q q q q

Trace over

q q q q q

Copy

q

Trace over

queen queen

Q q

Rr

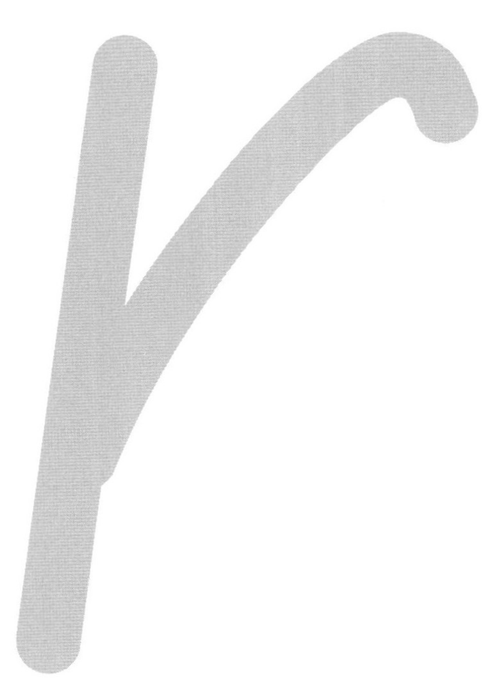

Channel

r r r r r

Trace over

r r r r r

Copy

r

Trace over

rabbit rabbit

Channel

S S S S S

Trace over

s s s s s

Copy

s

Trace over

snake snake

Ss

T t

Channel

 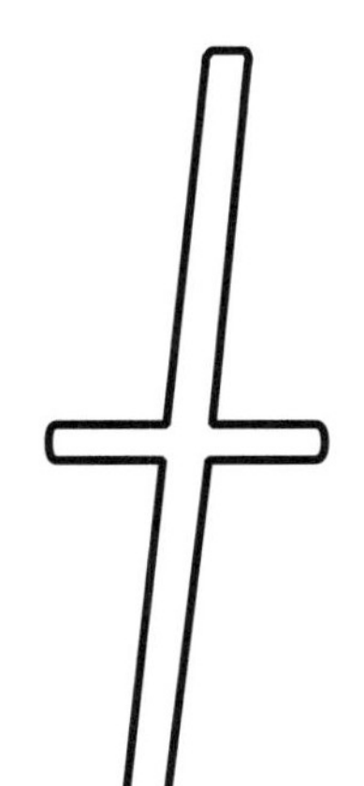 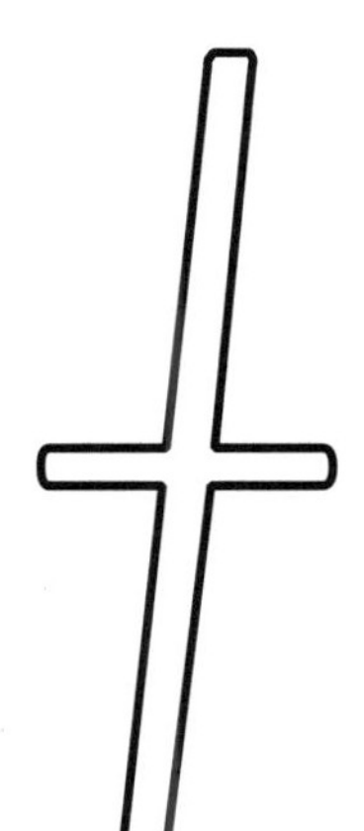  

Trace over

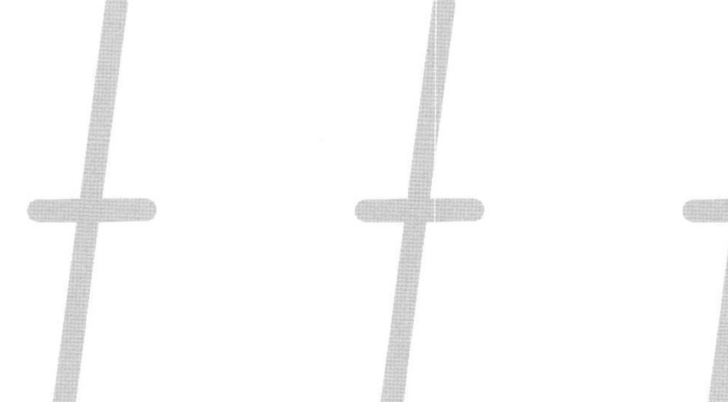  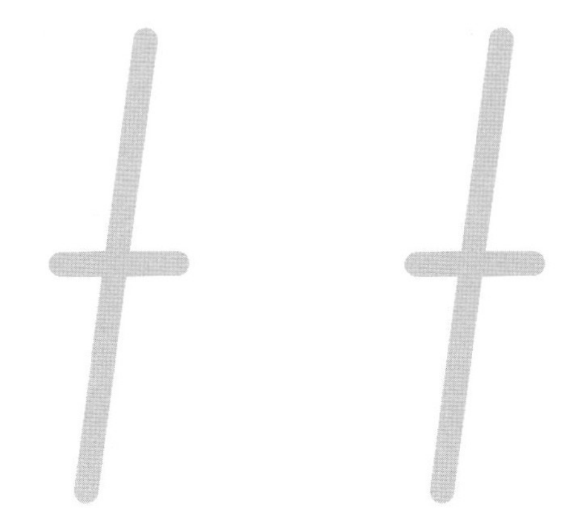

Copy

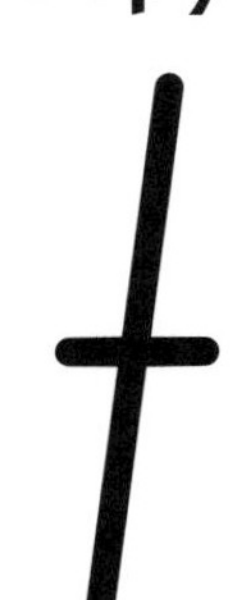

Trace over

tent

Channel

u u u u u

Trace over

u u u u u

Copy

u

Trace over

umbrella umbrella

Uu

Channel

v v v v v

Trace over

v v v v v

Copy

v

Trace over

vet vet vet

Channel

w w w w

Trace over

w w w w

Copy

w

Trace over

wand wand

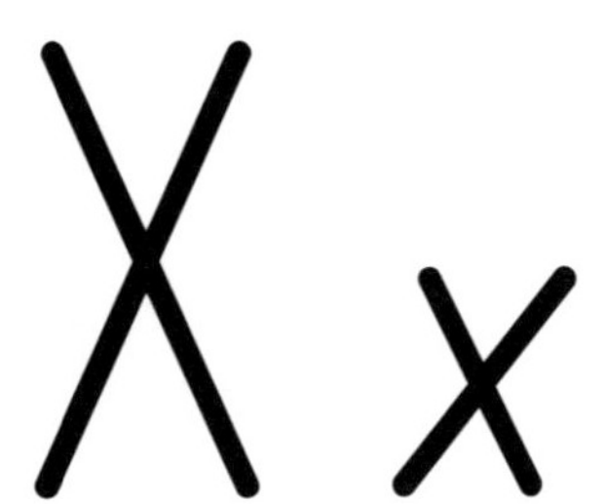

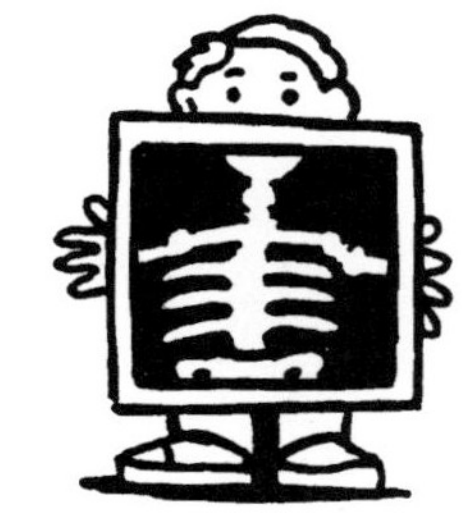

Channel

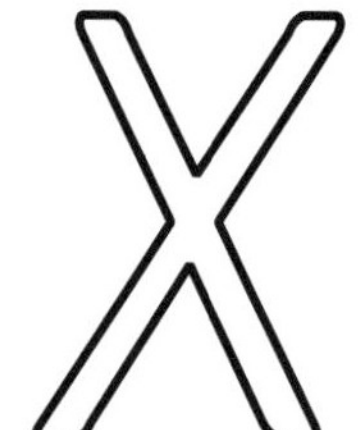    

Trace over

Copy

Trace over

Channel

y y y y y

Trace over

y y y y y

Copy

y

Trace over

yacht yacht

Yy

Z z

Channel

Z Z Z Z Z

Trace over

Z Z Z Z Z

Copy

Z

Trace over

zebra zebra

Find and trace over the letters of the alphabet. Colour the picture.